Make it in a Jar

Contents

Introduction

When you hear the terms "canning" or "preserving jars" and "mason jars," you may picture your grandmother in a flowery apron making jams and jellies. Generations of thrifty housewives, resourceful cooks, and gardeners have used these tempered glass beauties to put up the season's bounty to last through cold winters. But there's a trend afoot that has elevated these timeless vessels to do-it-all status, and they have become de rigueur in the modern kitchen. Simply put, canning jars are as retro-chic as they are undeniably practical.

They are attractive, come in a multitude of shapes and sizes, and can go from the pantry to the oven to the freezer to the refrigerator and back again. Use them as serving dishes and containers for lunch-box salads, cooking vessels for cakes, pies, even pizza, or as gift wrap for cookie and soup mixes. Bake mini cakes in small jars, tuck them in the freezer, and you'll always have a fancy dessert ready for when friends drop in unexpectedly. A jar of brownie or hot chocolate mix is the perfect present for a surprise Christmas guest. And batches of ready-to-mix pancake batter or ready-to-bake pasta with rich, creamy cheese sauce will make welcome treats for you and your family on busy days when you don't have time to cook a meal.

In short, what can't you do with a mason jar?

SELECTING JARS

If you plan to use jars for long-term storage or for cooking, be sure to buy authentic canning or mason jars, which are made of tempered, heat-resistant glass and come with lids that are equipped with channels coated with a sealing compound.

Some canning jar lids come in two pieces—a flat lid with a sealing rim and a metal band to hold it in place—while others are one-piece tops that screw right onto the jar.

Because we're not concerned here with preserving food for long-term keeping, any type of canning jars and lids will do well for our purposes.

For simplicity's sake, the recipes in this book use two sizes/shapes of jars: half-pint (8-fluid-ounce) widemouthed jars and pint (16-fluid-ounce) widemouthed jars. Buy a dozen of each of these sizes and you'll be prepared to make any of the recipes in this book.

We chose the widemouthed jars, which have straight sides instead of "shoulders," both because they are the most practical for use as serving vessels and because they are safe to use in the freezer. This is because liquid expands in all directions when it freezes, so even though there may be headspace above the shoulder of a regular-mouthed jar, the expansion of the liquid upon freezing could still break the glass.

Many of the recipes, however, will work equally well using normal-mouthed jars of the same size, as long as you're not planning to freeze them. If you already have a stash of canning jars you'd like to use, by all means go ahead and use them.

The most important thing is that the jars you choose are in good shape, and free from chips or cracks.

HOW TO USE CANNING JARS

Canning jars can be used in a myriad of different ways. In the first section of this book, we focus on dishes that are cooked and served right in the jars, from pizza and tarts to pies and cakes. These recipes use the jars' heat-resistant qualities and also take advantage of their usefulness in creating premeasured individual servings that are perfect for entertaining, packing for a picnic, or other on-the-go meals.

In the second section, we offer recipes that use the jars as serving dishes, showing off the food's beautiful layers of colors and textures; for example, Red Velvet Cupcakes layered with fluffy buttercream, Orange Panna Cotta with blackberry compote, Quinoa Salad with strawberries, almonds, scallions, and mint. Again, these dishes are ideal for entertaining, packing to eat on the go, or for giving.

In the third and final section, we use the jars as gift wrap for festive foods made specifically for giving, such as Red Lentil Soup Mix, Blueberry Pancake Mix, and ready-to-bake cookie dough.

Each of these applications takes advantage of the jars' see-through nature to show off interesting colors and textures in the food, as well as their unique ability to be used in a hot oven, to be chilled or frozen—even to be utilized for serving and transporting food.

TIPS FOR SUCCESS

Canning jars are surprisingly versatile, but they function a little differently from other cooking, serving, and storage containers. The recipes in this book have all been developed specifically for cooking, serving, or storing in canning jars, but if you're adapting a standard recipe to these applications, a little trial and error is unavoidable. Remember that things will cook at different rates in the jars than in your usual cooking vessels, and you may need to practice your layering technique a little to get just the visual impact you're hoping for.

To clean the jars, simply wash them by hand with dishwashing liquid in hot water, or put them in the dishwasher. If using the jars for long-term storage, it's a good idea to sterilize them, too, by submerging them in boiling water for 10–15 minutes before filling them.

When choosing recipes to make or serve in jars, think visually. Look for dishes that include a variety of colors and textures that can be layered in creative ways. Brightly colored fruit and vegetables and earthy nuts and seeds are all wonderful for creating stunning dishes.

When freezing food in jars, be sure to use the straight-sided, widemouthed jars and leave about half an inch of headroom at the top to allow for the expansion that takes place when liquid freezes. If you use normal-mouthed jars (with "shoulders"), you should fill them only about two-thirds full to avoid potential breakage.

Ready-to-bake cookie dough freezes well, and the cookies can be removed from the jar and put straight into a preheated oven for baking. Thaw other frozen foods, either by placing them in the refrigerator overnight or on a work surface for several hours. Cakes freeze well, too, but they should be frozen before frosting and should only be frosted after they have thawed.

In today's kitchen, canning jars function as far more than just utilitarian containers for long-term storage and preservation of fruit and vegetables. They offer a whimsical way to cook, serve, and make gifts of food that will delight your family and friends. Have fun with the process and be creative with the visual opportunities the jars afford.

Even your grandmother would be tickled pink to see the imaginative uses to which her boring old preserving jars are put these days!

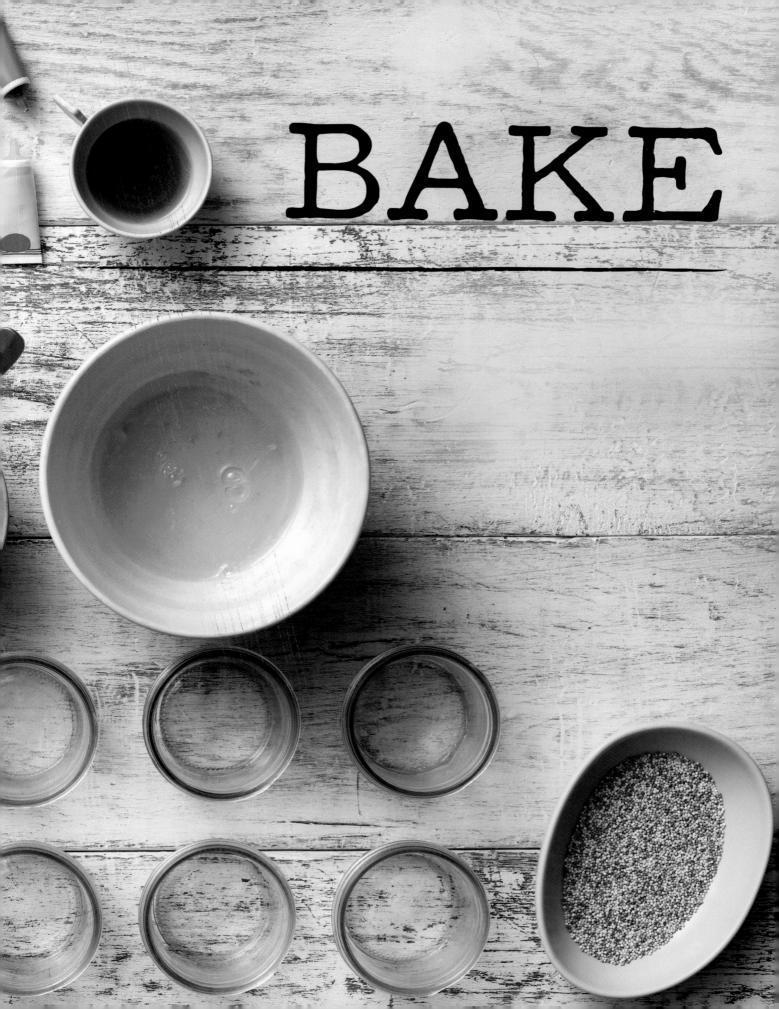

BAKE

Bake

Preserving jars are ideal vessels for baking individual, single servings. Because they are made of heat-resistant, tempered glass, the jars won't shatter in the oven and, in fact, baking in them is similar to baking in ceramic ramekins. And, as with ramekins, you save time on the cleanup by serving the food in the same vessel you've cooked it in. Even better, with canning jars you can put a lid on the food and take it along for a picnic in the park, or store it to use another day.

Perhaps best of all, canning jars really show off all the colors and textures of layered food, as in the rainbow cakes that have been all the rage in the blogosphere (and, of course, we've got a version here, too). But it's not just desserts that can be baked in jars. Try baked pasta dishes, such as Macaroni & Cheese, savory treats, such as our Asparagus Tart, or believe it or not, even pizza!

Many of these recipes can be stored in the refrigerator or freezer, either before or after cooking. Some foods, such as our Berry Cobbler or Macaroni & Cheese, are best frozen prior to cooking and then put, still frozen, directly into a hot oven, while others, such as cakes, are best stored after baking but before frosting. Thaw cakes for a few hours on a work surface and frost them just before serving. For your convenience, each recipe includes instructions for storing and thawing or reheating in the "Cook's Tips" section.

Cooking in jars isn't complicated, but it is a little different from cooking in the usual metal baking pans. Smaller portions will cook more quickly than larger ones. On the other hand, cooking in glass can take slightly longer than cooking in metal. Trial and error is par for the course when you're adapting a regular recipe to be cooked in jars. Of course, the recipes here have all been developed for, and tested in, jars, but you might want to plan for a test run if you're cooking a standard recipe in jars for the first time.

★ Rainbow Cakes

Preserving jars are perfect for showing off the pretty rainbow layers of these cute little cakes. A sweet cloud of frosting and colorful sugar sprinkles give them just the right finishing touch.

MAKES: 6 small jars

⬚⬚⬚⬚⬚⬚

◑ **PREP TIME** 45 minutes
COOK TIME 24 minutes

INGREDIENTS:

cooking spray, for greasing

1½ cups all-purpose flour

1½ teaspoons baking powder

¼ teaspoon salt

1 stick unsalted butter,
at room temperature

1 cup superfine sugar

2 teaspoons vanilla extract

4 large egg whites

½ cup milk

red, yellow, green, and blue
food coloring

rainbow sprinkles, to decorate

Frosting

3 egg whites

¾ cup sugar

2 sticks unsalted butter,
at room temperature

1 tablespoon vanilla extract

1. Preheat the oven to 350°F. Spray the insides of six half-pint (8-fluid-ounce) widemouthed canning jars with baking spray and place the jars on a jellyroll pan.

2. To make the cakes, put the flour, baking powder, and salt into a medium bowl and mix to combine.

3. Put the butter and sugar into a large bowl and beat with an electric mixer set on high speed until pale and fluffy. Add the vanilla extract, then add the egg whites, one at a time, beating after each addition until incorporated. Scrape down the side of the bowl, add half the flour mixture, and beat on medium speed until incorporated. Scrape down the side of the bowl, add the milk, and beat until incorporated. Scrape down the side of the bowl, add the remaining flour mixture, and beat until just incorporated.

4. Divide the batter among six small bowls. Color one bowl of batter red, using 8–10 drops of red food coloring. Color one bowl orange with 8 drops of yellow food coloring and 4 drops of red. Color one bowl yellow with 8 drops of yellow food coloring. Color one bowl green with 8 drops of green food coloring. Color one bowl blue with 8 drops of blue food coloring. Color one bowl purple with 8 drops of red food coloring and 4 drops of blue.

5. Spoon the batter into the prepared jars, one color at a time, starting with purple. Drop a tablespoonful into each jar and smooth it out with the back of the spoon so that it covers the entire bottom of the jar. Divide all the purple batter among the jars before moving on to the next color. Repeat with the blue, green, yellow, orange, and red batters, in that order, with the remaining bowls of batter. Bake in the preheated oven for 22–24 minutes, or until a toothpick inserted into the center of a cake comes out clean. Remove from the oven and let cool.

6. Meanwhile, to make the frosting, heat some water in the bottom of a double boiler until just simmering. Put the egg whites and sugar into the top of the double boiler and mix to combine (use a heatproof bowl set over a saucepan of simmering water if you don't have a double boiler). Set over the simmering water—the pan should be touching the water—

To store the cakes, follow the recipe until the baked cakes have cooled to room temperature. Do not prepare the frosting. Seal the jars with their lids and store the cakes in the refrigerator for up to 5 days, or in the freezer for up to 3 months. To serve, bring the cakes to room temperature, prepare the frosting as directed, and frost the cakes just before serving.

---

and whisk constantly for about 5 minutes, until the sugar has completely dissolved and the mixture is warm. Remove from the heat and, using an electric mixer, beat the mixture on high speed for about 5 minutes, until it holds stiff, glossy peaks. Add the butter, 1–2 tablespoons at a time, and beat until the mixture holds stiff peaks. Add the vanilla extract and beat until just combined. Spoon the frosting into a pastry bag fitted with your favorite tip.

7. When the cakes are completely cool, pipe the frosting onto them (if the cake has risen over the tops of the jars, remove some of it before topping with frosting). Top with the rainbow sprinkles and serve the cakes at room temperature.

3.

4.

5.

15

★ Cook's Tips ★

The uncooked cake batter can be kept in the refrigerator for 2–3 days
or in the freezer for up to 1 month. When you have put the batter
into the jars, seal them tightly with the lids, then place them in the
refrigerator or freezer. When ready to bake, proceed with the recipe.
If cooking from frozen, add 10–15 minutes to the cooking time.

These tart yet sweet cakes are perfectly delightful by themselves, but feel free to add a spoonful of lightly sweetened whipped cream if you're feeling indulgent.

Lemon Drizzle

MAKES: 6 small jars

PREP TIME 15 minutes
COOK TIME 30 minutes

INGREDIENTS:

1½ cups all-purpose flour

1½ teaspoons baking powder

¼ teaspoon salt

1½ sticks unsalted butter, at room temperature, plus extra for greasing

1 cup superfine sugar

2 large eggs

finely grated zest and juice of 1 lemon

sweetened whipped cream, to serve (optional)

Glaze
¼ cup sugar

juice of 1 lemon

1. Preheat the oven to 350°F. Grease six half-pint (8-fluid-ounce) widemouthed canning jars and place them on a jellyroll pan.

2. Put the flour, baking powder, and salt into a medium bowl and mix to combine.

3. Put the butter and sugar into a large bowl and beat with an electric mixer until pale and fluffy. Add the eggs, one at a time, beating after each addition until incorporated. Scrape down the side of the bowl, add the lemon zest and half the flour mixture, and beat until well-combined. Add the lemon juice and beat until incorporated. Scrape down the side of the bowl, add the remaining flour mixture, and mix until just incorporated.

4. Divide the batter among the prepared jars and bake in the preheated oven for about 30 minutes, or until a toothpick inserted in the center of a cake comes out clean.

5. Remove from the oven and immediately poke several holes into each cake using a chopstick or similar implement. To make the glaze, sprinkle 1 teaspoon of the sugar over the top of each cake. Add the lemon juice to the remaining sugar and stir until well-combined. Spoon the mixture over the tops of the cakes. Serve warm or at room temperature, with whipped cream, if using.

2.

4.

5.

★ S'mores Cakes

Preserving jars are a much neater and more convenient, but equally fun, way to serve this classic campfire treat.

MAKES: 8 small jars

⬠⬠⬠⬠⬠⬠⬠⬠

◔ **PREP TIME** 30 minutes
COOK TIME 47 minutes

INGREDIENTS:

Crust

8 graham crackers, broken into pieces

¼ cup plus 2 tablespoons sugar

1 stick unsalted butter, melted, plus extra for greasing

Cakes

1 cup all-purpose flour

¾ cup unsweetened cocoa powder

1½ teaspoons baking powder

¼ teaspoon salt

1 stick unsalted butter, at room temperature

1 cup superfine sugar

2 teaspoons vanilla extract

2 large eggs

½ cup heavy cream

¼ cup mini chocolate chips or chopped semisweet chocolate

32 large marshmallows

1. Preheat the oven to 350°F. Grease eight half-pint (8-fluid-ounce) widemouthed canning jars and place them on a jellyroll pan.

2. To make the crust, pulse the graham crackers in a food processor until they are reduced to coarse crumbs. Add the sugar and butter and pulse until just combined.

3. Spoon about 2 tablespoons of the mixture into each of the prepared jars, using your thumb to flatten it into the bottom and up the sides. Bake in the preheated oven for about 12 minutes, until beginning to turn golden brown.

4. To make the cakes, put the flour, cocoa powder, baking powder, and salt into a medium bowl.

5. Put the butter and sugar into a large bowl and cream together with an electric mixer. Add the vanilla extract, then add the eggs, one at a time, beating after each addition until incorporated. Add half the flour mixture and beat until incorporated. Add the cream and beat until incorporated. Add the remaining flour mixture and beat until incorporated. Stir in the chocolate chips.

6. Scoop the batter into the prepared jars and bake in the preheated oven for about 30 minutes, or until a toothpick inserted into the center of a cake comes out almost clean.

7. Increase the oven temperature to 475°F and press 4 marshmallows into the top of each jar. Return the cakes to the oven and bake for an additional 5–7 minutes, until the marshmallows are soft and lightly browned. Remove from the oven and let cool for a few minutes before serving. Serve warm.

3. 6. 7.

★ Cook's Tips ★

To store the cakes, follow the recipe up to step 6, then let the cakes cool to room temperature. Seal the jars with the lids and store in the refrigerator for up to 5 days, or in the freezer for up to 3 months. To serve, preheat the oven to 475°F, bring the cakes to room temperature, top with the marshmallows, and heat as directed until the marshmallows are golden.

★ Cook's Tips ★

Assemble the pies and freeze in the lidded jars for up to 3 months.
To serve, remove the lids and put the pies on a jellyroll pan in a
cold oven and heat the oven to 425°F. Bake for 20 minutes,
then reduce the temperature to 375°F and bake for an additional
35–40 minutes, until cooked through. Let cool.

It's hard to believe that so few ingredients can make a dessert so delicious, delightful, and portable.

Apple Pies

MAKES: 6 small jars

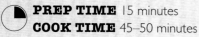

PREP TIME 15 minutes
COOK TIME 45–50 minutes

INGREDIENTS:

2 sheets chilled store-bought rolled dough pie crust, thawed if frozen

3 cups, diced, peeled, and cored Granny Smith apples

1 tablespoon lemon juice

⅓ cup granulated sugar

2 tablespoons light brown sugar

2 tablespoons all-purpose flour, plus extra for dusting

½ teaspoon ground cinnamon

⅛ teaspoon ground nutmeg

1. Preheat the oven to 425°F.

2. Roll out one piece of the dough on a lightly floured work surface and cut out six 3-inch circles. Place one circle in the bottom of each of six half-pint (8-fluid-ounce) widemouthed canning jars. Press the dough into the bottom and up the sides a little.

3. Put the apples and lemon juice into a large bowl and mix together, then add the granulated sugar, brown sugar, flour, cinnamon, and nutmeg and toss to coat the apples. Divide the mixture among the jars, packing it in as tightly as you can.

4. Roll out the remaining dough on a lightly floured work surface and cut out six 3-inch circles. Use a fork to pierce several small holes in each circle, then place one circle on top of the filling in each jar, tucking the edges inside the rims of the jars. Use the tines of a fork to create a decorative edge on the pastry, or use your fingers to fold and pleat it into a decorative border.

5. Place the jars on a jellyroll pan and bake in the preheated oven for about 15 minutes, then reduce the heat to 375°F and bake for an additional 30–35 minutes, until the filling is bubbling and the pastry is golden brown and crisp. Remove from the oven and let cool for 10–15 minutes. Serve warm.

3.

2.

5.

★ Cook's Tips ★

Prepare the cobbler up to the point of sprinkling on the sugar,
seal the jars with the lids, and store in the freezer for
up to 3 months. To serve, preheat the oven to 350°F, remove
the lids, and bake in the preheated oven for 40 minutes,
until cooked through.

This pretty and sweet mixed berry treat is a great way to enjoy summer's bounty all-year-round.

Berry Cobblers

MAKES: 8 small jars

PREP TIME 15 minutes
COOK TIME 35 minutes

INGREDIENTS:

4 cups mixed berries
(any combination of blackberries, raspberries, blueberries, and strawberries), thawed and drained, if frozen

½ cup sugar

1 tablespoon lemon juice

2 tablespoons cornstarch

Topping

1 cup all-purpose flour

2 tablespoons sugar

½ teaspoon cinnamon

pinch of salt

½ stick unsalted butter

¼ cup heavy cream

1 large egg

4 teaspoons raw brown sugar

1. Preheat the oven to 350°F.

2. Put the berries, sugar, lemon juice, and cornstarch into a medium bowl and mix to combine. Divide the mixture among eight half-pint (8-fluid-ounce) widemouthed canning jars.

3. To make the topping, put the flour, sugar, cinnamon, and salt into a food processor and pulse to combine. Add the butter and pulse until the mixture resembles coarse crumbs. Add the cream and egg and process until the mixture comes together into a loose, sticky ball.

4. Spoon the topping onto the berry mixture, dividing it among the jars. Sprinkle the brown sugar over the top and bake in the preheated oven for about 35 minutes, or until the topping is golden brown and cooked through. Serve warm.

★ Cook's Tips ★

Prepare the macaroni and cheese up to the point of adding
the bread-crumb topping. Seal the jars with their lids and freeze
for up to 3 months. To serve, preheat the oven to 375°F. Remove
the lids and bake them in the preheated oven for 30 minutes
until cooked through.

Bubbling away in see-through jars, this rich, creamy pasta dish with its crunchy bread-crumb topping is irresistible.

Macaroni & Cheese

MAKES: 8 small jars or 4 large jars

⬤ **PREP TIME** 15 minutes
  COOK TIME 35 minutes

INGREDIENTS:

oil, for greasing

1 pound dried elbow macaroni

1 stick unsalted butter

2 tablespoons all-purpose flour

1¼ cups light cream

3 cups coarsely shredded sharp cheddar cheese

1 cup shredded fontina cheese

2 teaspoons sweet or smoked paprika

½ teaspoon salt

½ teaspoon pepper

Topping

1 cup dried bread crumbs

3 tablespoons unsalted butter, melted

⅓ cup freshly grated Parmesan cheese

1. Preheat the oven to 375°F and oil eight half-pint (8-fluid-ounce) or four 1-pint (16-fluid-ounce) widemouthed canning jars and place them on a jellyroll pan.

2. Cook the pasta according to the package directions, until tender but still firm to the bite. Drain, reserving ½ cup of the cooking water.

3. Melt the butter in a large saucepan. Add the flour and whisk over medium heat until the mixture is just beginning to brown and gives off a nutty aroma. Reduce the heat to low and stir in the cream until fully incorporated. Remove the pan from the heat and stir in the cheddar cheese and fontina cheese until completely melted. If the sauce is too thick, add a little of the reserved pasta cooking water, 1 tablespoon at a time, stirring until incorporated. Add more water, if needed, to achieve the desired consistency. Stir in the paprika, salt, and pepper. Add the pasta and stir to coat well. Divide the pasta among the jars.

4. To make the topping, combine the bread crumbs, melted butter, and Parmesan cheese. Spoon over the top of the pasta, dividing equally among the jars.

5. Bake the jars in the preheated oven for about 25 minutes, until the mixture is bubbling and the topping is golden brown. Let stand for 1–2 minutes before serving.

Focaccia is ideal for cooking in single servings with a crisp, golden crust surrounding a soft, fluffy interior.

Olive, Sun-Dried Tomato & Sage Focaccia

MAKES: 12 small jars

PREP TIME 15 minutes, plus 2 hours 15 minutes to rise
COOK TIME 35 minutes

INGREDIENTS:

1¾ cups lukewarm water

2¼ teaspoons active dry yeast

1 tablespoon sugar

4½ cups white bread flour, plus extra if needed and for dusting

1 tablespoon salt

1 cup olive oil, plus extra for oiling and drizzling

½ cup chopped Kalamata olives

2 tablespoons chopped sun-dried tomatoes

1 tablespoon chopped fresh sage

coarse salt, for sprinkling

1. Put the water into a large mixing bowl and sprinkle the yeast and sugar on top. Let stand in a warm place for 15–20 minutes, or until the mixture is foaming.

2. Add the flour, salt, and half the oil to the yeast mixture and mix with an electric mixer on low speed until the dough begins to come together. Knead the dough for about 5 minutes, until it is smooth and springy. The dough should be fairly wet and sticky, but if it is too wet to handle, add more flour, 1 tablespoon at a time, until the desired consistency is achieved.

3. Turn out the dough onto a lightly floured board and knead in the olives, tomatoes, and sage until thoroughly combined. Form the dough into a ball and put it into a large, oiled bowl. Turn the ball until it is coated with oil. Loosely cover with a clean dish towel and let stand in a warm place for about 1 hour, or until doubled in size.

4. Put 1 teaspoon of the remaining oil in each of 12 half-pint (8-fluid-ounce) widemouthed canning jars, turning the jars so that the insides are completely coated. Divide the dough into 12 balls and place a ball in each of the prepared jars. Turn the balls in the jars until they are coated with oil. Put the jars on a jellyroll pan and set aside for about 1 hour, or until doubled in size.

5. Meanwhile, preheat the oven to 425°F. Drizzle the dough balls with a little oil and sprinkle with coarse salt. Bake in the preheated oven for about 35 minutes, or until the tops are puffed and golden brown. Serve the focaccia warm or at room temperature.

1.　　4.　　5.

★ Cook's Tips ★

The focaccia can be covered with aluminum foil and stored at room
temperature for 1-2 days. To keep for longer, remove from the jars,
place in freezer bags, and freeze for up to 3 months. Bring to room
temperature before serving.

Children and adults alike will be delighted by these individual pizzas made with a simple tomato sauce, creamy fresh mozzarella, and fresh basil.

Pizza Margherita

MAKES: 12 small jars

PREP TIME 45 minutes, plus 1¼ hours to rise
COOK TIME 50 minutes

INGREDIENTS:

1¾ cups lukewarm water

2¼ teaspoons active dry yeast

1 tablespoon sugar

4½ cups white bread flour, plus extra for dusting

1 tablespoon salt

½ cup olive oil, plus extra for oiling and drizzling

1 pound fresh mozzarella cheese, thinly sliced

handful of fresh basil, torn

coarse salt, for sprinkling

Sauce

1 tablespoon unsalted butter

1 tablespoon olive oil

2 garlic cloves, finely chopped

2 shallots, diced

1 (28-ounce) can of San Marzano tomatoes, diced, with their can juices

¼ teaspoon red pepper flakes

salt and pepper

1. Pour the water into a large mixing bowl and sprinkle the yeast and sugar on top. Let stand in a warm place for 15–20 minutes, or until the mixture is foaming.

2. Add the flour, salt, and half the oil to the yeast mixture and mix with an electric mixer on low speed until the dough begins to come together. Knead the dough for about 5 minutes, or until it is smooth and springy. The dough should be fairly wet and sticky, but if it is too wet to handle, add more flour, 1 tablespoon at a time, until the desired consistency is achieved.

3. Turn out the dough onto a lightly floured board and knead for 1–2 minutes, dusting with a little flour if needed. Form the dough into a ball and put it into a large, oiled bowl. Turn the ball until it is coated with oil. Loosely cover with a clean dish towel and let stand in a warm place for about 1 hour, or until doubled in size.

4. Meanwhile, make the sauce. Heat the butter and oil in a medium saucepan until the butter is melted and the oil is hot. Add the garlic and shallots and cook, stirring, for about 4 minutes, until soft. Add the tomatoes, ½ teaspoon of salt, ½ teaspoon of pepper, and the red pepper flakes and bring to a boil. Reduce the heat to medium-low and simmer for about 45 minutes, or until thick. Using an immersion blender or food processor, puree the sauce until smooth. Add salt and pepper to taste.

5. Oil 12 half-pint (8-fluid-ounce) widemouthed canning jars and put them on a jellyroll pan. Preheat the oven to 400°F.

6. Divide the dough into two pieces. Return one piece to the bowl and cover with the dish towel. Divide the other piece into 12 balls. Roll out or press each ball into a 4-inch circle and place one circle in the bottom of each of the prepared jars, pressing it into the bottom and up the sides. Bake in the preheated oven for about 20–25 minutes, until the crusts are light brown and crisp.

7. Make 12 more circles with the remaining dough. Remove the jars
from the oven (do not turn off the oven) and spoon sauce into each on
top of the pizza crusts, filling each jar with 1½–2 inches of sauce. Top the
sauce with the mozzarella cheese and the basil. Top with another pizza
crust circle, pushing it down into the jar. Drizzle a little oil over the top
and sprinkle with coarse salt. Return to the oven and bake for about
25–30 minutes, until the top is brown and crisp. Serve hot.

3.

4.

7.

31

★ Cook's Tips ★

The tarts can be stored in the freezer, unbaked, for up to
3 months. Assemble the tart with the uncooked pastry. Seal the
jars with their lids and store in the freezer. To serve, remove
the lids, preheat the oven to 425°F, and bake the frozen pies for
20-25 minutes, or until cooked through.

Layers of golden pastry conceal a rich, tangy goat cheese custard studded with succulent asparagus.

Asparagus Tarts

MAKES: 8 small jars

 PREP TIME 15 minutes
COOK TIME 30 minutes

INGREDIENTS:

2 sheets chilled store-bought rolled dough pie crust, thawed if frozen

flour, for dusting

1 pound asparagus, cut into 1-inch pieces

⅓ cup water

4 eggs

4 ounces goat cheese

1⅓ cups light cream

¾ teaspoon salt

½ teaspoon pepper

finely grated rind of 1 lemon

1. Preheat the oven to 425°F.

2. Roll out one piece of dough on a lightly floured work surface and cut out eight 3-inch circles. Place one circle in the bottom of each of eight half-pint (8-fluid-ounce) widemouthed canning jars. Use a fork to pierce several holes in each circle. Put the jars on a jellyroll pan and bake in the preheated oven for about 15 minutes, until the pastry is light brown. Remove from the oven, but do not turn off the oven.

3. Meanwhile, put the asparagus into a medium microwave-safe bowl with the water. Cover with plastic wrap and heat on high for 1–2 minutes, or until just tender.

4. Put the eggs, cheese, cream, salt, pepper, and lemon rind into a bowl and beat with an electric mixer until smooth. Divide the mixture among the jars, ladling it over the pastry. Divide the asparagus among the jars, arranging it on the custard in a single layer.

5. Roll out the remaining pastry and cut out eight 3-inch circles. Use a fork to pierce several holes in each circle, then place one circle on top of the filling in each jar, tucking the edges inside the rims of the jars. Bake in the preheated oven for about 15 minutes, until the filling is set and the pastry lid is golden brown and crisp. Let cool for a few minutes, then serve.

2. **4.** **4.**

MAKE

Make

As the photos on these pages show, canning jars make wonderfully attractive serving vessels and lend a fashionable air of retro-chic to a party table. Fill them with layers of colorful foods—from rainbow-colored salads to layered desserts—for a stunning presentation that will be a talking point among your guests. Better still, filled jars can be lidded and taken along for a picnic, boat, or car journey, bake sale, a day at the office, or any other time you want to take your meal with you.

For the best results, give some thought to how your jars will look before you begin filling them, and think also about how the ingredients will interact with each other in the jar. For instance, when making salads, dressing should always go in first, with sturdy ingredients going in just on top of the dressing and more delicate ingredients, such as salad greens, at the top of the jar. This way, the dressing won't make the lettuce soggy and your salad will remain fresh and crisp in the refrigerator. Just before serving, with the lid still on, you can shake your jar of salad to distribute the dressing throughout. *Voilà!* Tossed salad in an instant.

Think, too, about how your ingredients will look when layered in the jar. Put contrasting colors and textures next to each other for the greatest visual impact. Layer ingredients neatly and shake or tap the jars to even out the layers as you work. To keep the layers and the jar rims neat, use a widemouthed funnel, an ice cream scoop, a ladle, or even a pastry bag to fill the jars.

★ Red Velvet Cakes

The rich red hue of this chocolatey cake is set off beautifully against layers of snow-white buttercream.

MAKES: 6 small jars

◻◻◻◻◻◻

PREP TIME 20 minutes
COOK TIME 20 minutes

INGREDIENTS:

1½ cups all-purpose flour

3 tablespoons unsweetened cocoa powder

¼ teaspoon salt

1 stick unsalted butter, at room temperature, plus extra for greasing

1½ cups superfine sugar

1 teaspoon vanilla extract

2 large eggs

⅔ cup buttermilk

1 tablespoon red gel food coloring

1 teaspoon apple cider vinegar

1 teaspoon baking soda

chocolate shavings, mini chocolate chips, or chocolate sprinkles, to decorate

Frosting

3 egg whites

¾ cup sugar

2 sticks unsalted butter, at room temperature

1 tablespoon vanilla extract

1. Preheat the oven to 350°F and grease a 9 x 13-inch cake pan.

2. Put the flour, cocoa powder, and salt into a medium bowl and mix to combine.

3. Put the butter and sugar into a large bowl and beat with an electric mixer set on high speed, until pale and fluffy. Add the vanilla extract, then add the eggs, one at a time, beating after each addition until incorporated. Add half the flour mixture and beat on medium speed until incorporated. Scrape down the side of the bowl, add the buttermilk and food coloring, and beat until incorporated. Scrape down the side of the bowl, add the remaining flour mixture, and beat until just incorporated. Put the vinegar and baking soda into a small bowl and stir to combine; wait until the foaming subsides, then add to the batter and beat until incorporated.

4. Transfer the batter to the prepared pan, smoothing the top with a spatula. Bake in the preheated oven for about 20 minutes, until a toothpick inserted into the center comes out clean. Remove from the oven and let cool for several minutes, then turn out onto a cooling rack to cool completely.

5. To make the frosting, heat some water in the bottom of a double boiler until just simmering. Put the egg whites and sugar into the top of the double boiler (or use a heatproof bowl over a saucepan of simmering water) and mix to combine. Set over the simmering water and whisk constantly for about 5 minutes, until the sugar has completely dissolved and the mixture is warm.

6. Remove from the heat and, using an electric mixer, beat the mixture on high speed for about 5 minutes, until it holds stiff, glossy peaks. Add the butter, 1–2 tablespoons at a time, and beat until the mixture holds stiff peaks. Add the vanilla extract and beat until just combined.

7. Using a 2½-inch round cookie cutter, cut 12 circles out of the cake. Place one circle in the bottom of each of six half-pint (8-fluid-ounce) widemouthed canning jars. Top each cake circle with a large spoonful of the frosting and then a second circle of cake. Finish with another large spoonful of frosting, smoothing the top with the back of the spoon. Sprinkle with chocolate shavings and serve immediately.

Rich devil's food cake, creamy peanut butter frosting, and a dark chocolate shell combine to make one irresistible dessert.

Chocolate Peanut Butter Cupcakes

MAKES: 6 large jars or 12 small jars

PREP TIME 30 minutes
COOK TIME 20 minutes

INGREDIENTS:

1 cup all-purpose flour

¾ cup unsweetened cocoa powder

1½ teaspoons baking powder

¼ teaspoon salt

1 stick unsalted butter, at room temperature, plus extra for greasing

1 cup superfine sugar

2 teaspoons vanilla extract

2 large eggs

½ cup heavy cream

Frosting & topping

1 stick unsalted butter, softened

½ cup creamy peanut butter

1½–2½ cups confectioners' sugar

2 tablespoons milk

pinch of salt

8 ounces dark coating chocolate or 1¼ cups semisweet chocolate chips

2 tablespoons vegetable oil

1. Preheat the oven to 350° and grease a 9 × 13-inch cake pan.

2. To make the cake, put the flour, cocoa powder, baking powder, and salt into a medium bowl.

3. Put the butter and sugar into a large bowl and beat with an electric mixer set on high speed for several minutes, until pale yellow and fluffy. Add the vanilla extract, then add the eggs, one at a time, beating after each addition until incorporated. Add half the flour mixture and beat on medium speed until incorporated. Scrape down the side of the bowl, add the cream, and beat until incorporated. Scrape down the side of the bowl, add the remaining flour mixture, and beat until just incorporated.

4. Spoon the batter into the prepared pan, smoothing the top. Bake in the preheated oven for about 20 minutes, or until a toothpick inserted into the center comes out clean. Let cool in the pan for 1–2 minutes, then transfer to a cooling rack to cool completely.

5. To make the frosting, put the butter and peanut butter into a medium bowl and beat with an electric mixer until creamy. Add 1½ cups of the confectioners' sugar, the milk, and salt. Beat together until well combined. Gradually beat in more confectioners' sugar until the desired consistency has been achieved.

6. Place the cake on a flat surface and use a 2½–inch circle cookie cutter to cut out 12 circles.

7. If using 1 pint (16-fluid-ounce jars), place one circle of cake in the bottom of each of six widemouthed jars. Spoon 2–3 tablespoons of frosting on top, smoothing with the back of a spoon. Top the frosting with a second layer of cake and top that with a second layer of frosting, smoothing the top.

8. If making 12 half-pint (8-fluid-ounce) jars, layer them with one circle of cake and one layer of frosting.

9. To make the topping, put the coating chocolate and oil into a small microwave-safe bowl and heat on Low for 30 seconds at a time, until the chocolate has mostly melted. Stir vigorously with a fork until the chocolate is completely melted.

10. Spoon the chocolate over the tops of the frosted cakes so that the frosting is completely covered in chocolate. Chill in the refrigerator for 5–10 minutes, until the chocolate is set. Serve at room temperature.

★ Cook's Tips ★

Refrigerate the cakes in the covered jars for up
to 3 days, or freeze them for up to 3 months.
Bring to room temperature before serving.

★ Cook's Tips ★

The panna cottas will keep, covered, in the refrigerator
for several days. The compote can be added to the panna cottas once
they have set or just before serving.

This light and refreshing pudding is as delicious as it is beautiful. Any type of berry—strawberries, blueberries, raspberries, or a combination—will work just as well for the compote.

Orange Panna Cotta

MAKES: 6 small jars

PREP TIME 15 minutes, plus at least 4 hours to chill
COOK TIME 10 minutes

INGREDIENTS:

3 tablespoons freshly squeezed orange juice

2¼ teaspoons gelatin

4 cups milk

½ cup sugar

1 teaspoon vanilla extract

2 teaspoons finely grated orange rind

Blackberry compote

1½ cups fresh or frozen blackberries

¼ cup water

¼ cup sugar

2 tablespoons lemon juice

1. Put the orange juice into a small bowl and sprinkle the gelatin on top. Set aside until the gelatin has absorbed the liquid.

2. In a medium saucepan, combine the milk, sugar, and vanilla extract, set over medium-high heat, and bring to a simmer, stirring to incorporate the sugar. Remove from the heat and stir in the orange rind and the gelatin mixture. Whisk until the gelatin has fully dissolved. Divide the mixture among six half-pint (8-fluid-ounce) widemouthed canning jars. Let cool to room temperature, then seal the jars with their lids and refrigerate for at least 4 hours, until set.

3. To make the compote, put all the ingredients into a medium saucepan set over medium-high heat and stir to combine. Bring to a boil, then reduce the heat to medium-low and simmer until the sugar has dissolved, the liquid is beginning to thicken, and the fruit is beginning to break down. Remove from the heat and let cool to room temperature.

4. Remove the lids from the jars of panna cotta, spoon the compote over the tops, and serve immediately.

1.   2.   3.

> Refrigerator cakes are perfect for single-serving canning jars.

Gingersnap Icebox Cakes

MAKES: 6 small jars

PREP TIME 15 minutes, plus 4 hours to chill
COOK TIME No cooking

INGREDIENTS:

2 cups heavy cream

¼ cup sugar

finely grated rind and juice of 1 lemon

36 gingersnaps, 12 broken in half

1½ ounces chopped candied ginger, to decorate

1. Put the cream into a large bowl and whip until it holds stiff peaks. Add the sugar and lemon rind and juice and beat until combined.

2. Spoon about 2 tablespoons of the mixture into the bottom of each of six half-pint (8-fluid-ounce) widemouthed canning jars. Top each cream layer with 1½ cookies in a single layer.

3. Spoon another 2 tablespoons of the cream mixture on top of the cookies, and top with another 1½ cookies. Repeat until there are 4 layers of cookies.

4. Finish with a layer of cream. Wipe the rims of the jars clean and seal the jars with their lids. Chill in the refrigerator for at least 4 hours.

5. Just before serving, remove the lids and sprinkle the ginger over the tops.

★ Cook's Tips ★

The cakes will keep in the refrigerator for up to 3 days or in
the freezer for up to 3 months. Remove the frozen cakes from
the freezer and refrigerate for at least 4 hours before serving.
Sprinkle the ginger on top just before serving.

★ Cook's Tips ★

Banana splits can be frozen for up to 3 months. Follow the
recipe up to the addition of the third layer of ice cream. Seal
the jars with their lids and freeze. Remove from the freezer
about 10 minutes before serving. Add the chocolate sauce,
whipped cream, nuts, and cherries just before serving.

Banana Splits

Three flavors of ice cream alternate with layers of sliced bananas under a drizzle of rich chocolate sauce. Whipped cream, nuts, and a cherry on top make the perfect finish.

MAKES: 6 large jars

PREP TIME 15 minutes
COOK TIME 5 minutes

INGREDIENTS:

6 scoops (1 pint) chocolate ice cream

6 scoops (1 pint) vanilla ice cream

6 scoops (1 pint) strawberry ice cream

6 ripe bananas, sliced

Chocolate sauce
4 ounces semisweet chocolate, chopped

½ cup heavy cream

2 tablespoons unsalted butter, diced

pinch of salt

To decorate
2 cups whipped cream

3 tablespoons chopped nuts

6 maraschino cherries

1. Remove the ice cream from the freezer and let soften for about 10 minutes.

2. Meanwhile, to make the chocolate sauce, put the chocolate, cream, butter, and salt into a microwave-safe bowl. Heat on low for 30 seconds, or until the cream is hot and the chocolate has mostly melted. Stir vigorously until the chocolate has completely melted and is well incorporated with the other ingredients. Let cool for a few minutes.

3. Place one-third of the slices from one banana in the bottom of each of six half-pint (8-fluid-ounce) widemouthed canning jars. Put a scoop of strawberry ice cream into each jar, flattening it with the back of the spoon. Add a second layer of banana slices and top with a scoop of chocolate ice cream. Top with a third layer of banana slices, then add a scoop of vanilla ice cream.

4. Drizzle chocolate sauce over the top, letting it drip down the sides. Top each jar with whipped cream, a sprinkling of nuts, and a maraschino cherry and serve immediately.

2.

3.

3.

★ Cook's Tips ★

The simple syrup will keep indefinitely, stored in a lidded jar
in the refrigerator. This recipe can easily make smaller cocktails.
Use 12 half-pint (8-fluid-ounce) jars and halve the quantity of each
of the ingredients for the individual cocktails.

Don't get stuck tending bar at your next barbecue. Mix up cocktails in mason jars and stash them in a bucket of ice so that guests can simply help themselves.

Mojitos to Go

MAKES: 6 large jars

PREP TIME 10 minutes
COOK TIME 5 minutes

INGREDIENTS:

30 fresh mint leaves, plus extra to serve

7½ cups club soda

1¾–2¼ cups (12–18 ounces) light rum

1 cup lime juice

ice cubes, and lime wedges, to serve

Mint simple syrup

1½ cups sugar

1½ cups water

scant handful of fresh mint leaves, torn into pieces

1. To prepare the simple syrup, put the sugar and water into a saucepan set over medium-high heat and bring to a boil. Reduce the heat to medium and cook, stirring, for about 2 minutes, or until the sugar has completely dissolved. Remove from the heat, stir in the mint let, cover, and let steep for about 1 hour. Strain the syrup into a jar, discarding the mint leaves, and store, covered, in the refrigerator until ready to use.

2. To make the cocktails, put ⅓ cup simple syrup in each of the six 1-pint (16-fluid-ounce) mason jars. Add five fresh mint leaves to each jar, crinkling them with your fingers before you add them. Muddle together the mint and simple syrup using the back of a spoon or a cocktail muddler. Add 1¼ cups club soda, ¼–⅓ cup (2–3 ounces) rum, and 3 tablespoons of lime juice to each jar. Seal the jars with their lids and shake very gently to mix. Store the jars in the refrigerator, cooler, or bucket of ice until ready to serve. Serve cold, decorated with fresh mint sprigs, ice cubes, and lime wedges.

1. **2.** **2.**

Roasted Beet & Arugula Salad

Deep red beets at the bottom, bright candied orange zest at the top, and fresh green arugula in the middle make for a beautifully refreshing salad.

MAKES: 6 large jars

⏱ **PREP TIME** 15 minutes
COOK TIME 2 hours 40 minutes, plus overnight to crisp the orange zest

INGREDIENTS:

Candied Orange Zest
2 large navel oranges

½ cup sugar

Vinaigrette
¼ cup white wine vinegar

2 tablespoons Dijon mustard

2 teaspoons honey

1 teaspoon salt

½ teaspoon pepper

¼ cup olive oil

Salad
6 beets

6 handfuls arugula

⅔ cup crumbled blue cheese

2 tablespoons walnuts or pecans

1. To make the candied orange zest, use a vegetable peeler to remove the zest from the oranges, leaving all the white pith behind. Cut the zest into ¼-inch-wide strips. Put them into a small saucepan, cover with cold water, and bring to a boil over medium-high heat. Reduce the heat to medium and simmer for 5 minutes. Remove from the heat and drain in a colander.

2. Put the sugar into the pan with ½ cup water and heat over medium heat until the sugar has completely dissolved. Add the drained zest to the pan and bring to simmering point. Reduce the heat to low and simmer gently for about 20 minutes, or until the zest is translucent.

3. Meanwhile, preheat the oven to its lowest setting and line a baking sheet with parchment paper.

4. Remove the zest from the pan, using a slotted spoon, letting the excess liquid drain off. Spread the zest on the prepared baking sheet in a single layer and place in the preheated oven for 1 hour. Turn off the oven, but do not remove the zest. Let cook in the oven overnight, or for up to 24 hours, until it is crisp.

5. To make the salad, preheat the oven to 475°F.

6. Wrap each beet in aluminum foil and bake in the preheated oven for about 1 hour 15 minutes, until tender. Remove from the oven and let cool. When cool enough to handle, slip off the skins and dice the beets.

7. To make the vinaigrette, combine the vinegar, mustard, honey, salt, and pepper in a small bowl and whisk to combine. Add the oil and whisk until emulsified.

8. Toss half the dressing with the beets and toss the remainder with the arugula. Divide the beets among six 1-pint (16-fluid-ounce) widemouthed canning jars. Add the dressed arugula, then a layer of cheese and a layer of nuts. Garnish each jar with a sprinkling of candied orange zest and serve immediately.

1.   7.   8.

★ Cook's Tips ★

The salads can be stored in the refrigerator for up to 3 days. To make them ahead of time, divide all the dressing among the jars, then layer in the beets, arugula, cheese, nuts, and zest. Seal the jars with their lids and refrigerate for up to 3 days. Shake well before serving to distribute the dressing.

★ Cook's Tips ★

These salads can be made up to 3 days ahead.
Seal the finished salads with their lids and store
in the refrigerator. Bring to room temperature
before serving.

Canning jars are the perfect way to show off the bright, fresh colors of this hearty salad.

Quinoa Salads

MAKES: 12 small jars or 6 large jars

PREP TIME 15 minutes
COOK TIME 15 minutes

INGREDIENTS:

1½ cups red or golden quinoa

4 scallions, thinly sliced

2 cups fresh strawberries, sliced

¾ cup crumbled fresh goat cheese

½ cup chopped, roasted unsalted pistachio nuts

handful of fresh mint leaves, chopped

Dressing

⅓ cup lemon juice

1 teaspoon honey

1 teaspoon Dijon mustard

½ teaspoon salt

½ teaspoon pepper

⅔ cup olive oil

1. Cook the quinoa according to the package instructions and let cool.

2. To make the dressing, combine the lemon juice, honey, mustard, salt, and pepper in a small jar or bowl and shake or whisk to combine. Add the oil and shake or whisk vigorously until emulsified.

3. Toss 3 tablespoons of the dressing with the cooked quinoa.

4. To make the salads, place 1 tablespoon of the dressing in each of twelve half-pint (8-fluid-ounce) widemouthed canning jars, or place 2 tablespoons of the dressing in each of six 1-pint (16-fluid-ounce jars). Add a layer of quinoa to each jar. Add the scallions, then a layer of strawberries, then a layer of cheese, then a layer of nuts, and finally top with mint. Spoon a little more dressing over the top and serve immediately.

1.   4.   4.

TAKE

Take

With the do-it-yourself trend going strong at the moment, homemade gifts are more fashionable than they've ever been. And what could be better than a homemade gift of something delicious? Canning jars are ideal gift packaging for ready-to-bake cookies or easy-to-finish mixes for soup, pretzels, brownies, muffins, pancakes, and much, much more.

For great food gifts in jars, use clean, unchipped jars with lids that seal tightly. Be sure to include storage instructions, which can be found in the "Cook's Tips" section of each recipe, as well as information for how to bake or make the final product (also included with each recipe). Dry mixes will keep indefinitely in a cool, dark place, and ready-to-bake cookie dough can be frozen.

Filling the jars is only half the fun. Get creative with pretty gift tags, labels, cooking instructions, and ribbons. Cover the tops with decorative paper or squares of colorful cloth. Your food gifts will be as beautiful as they are appetizing.

And just think how the recipients will delight in the gift when they first receive it, then rejoice once more when their house is filled with the smell of hot lentil soup, fresh-baked pretzels, brownies, or cookies.

Chocolate Chip Coconut Cookies

The classic chocolate chip cookie gets a makeover. Sweet shredded coconut adds an addictive chewiness, while puffed rice cereal gives some unexpected crunch.

MAKES: 6 large jars, each with 12 cookies

PREP TIME 20 minutes, plus at least 4 hours to freeze
COOK TIME No cooking

INGREDIENTS:

2 cups all-purpose flour

1½ teaspoons baking soda

¾ teaspoon salt

1½ sticks unsalted butter, at room temperature

¾ cup packed light brown sugar

¾ cup granulated sugar

1 tablepoon vanilla extract

2 large eggs

3 cups puffed rice cereal

1½ cups dry sweetened coconut

1½ cups mini semisweet chocolate chips

1. Line two large baking sheets with parchment paper. Put the flour, baking soda, and salt into a medium bowl and mix to combine.

2. Put the butter, brown sugar, and granulated sugar into a large bowl and beat with an electric mixer until pale and fluffy. Scrape down the side of the bowl, add the vanilla extract, then add the eggs and beat until incorporated. Add the flour mixture and beat until well combined. Stir in the rice cereal, coconut, and chocolate chips.

3. Use your hands to form the dough into 1-inch balls and place them on the prepared baking sheets. You should have 72 dough balls. Place the sheets in the freezer for at least 4 hours or overnight, until the balls are completely frozen.

4. Place 12 frozen dough balls in each of six 1 pint (16-fluid-ounce) widemouthed canning jars. Attach a gift tag to each jar with the following instructions:

How to bake Chocolate Chip Coconut Cookies

Keep frozen until required. Preheat the oven to 350°F and place the frozen dough balls on an ungreased cookie sheet, spaced about 2 inches apart. Bake in the preheated oven for about 12 minutes, until the cookies have spread out and are beginning to brown around the edges. Remove from the oven and let cool on the sheet for 1–2 minutes. Using a spatula, transfer the cookies to a cooling rack to cool. Serve warm or at room temperature.

★ Cook's Tips ★

The frozen dough will keep in the freezer,
tightly sealed, for up to 3 months.

2.

4.

5.

★ Cook's Tips ★

The cookies will keep in the freezer,
tightly sealed, for up to 3 months.

These spicy gingersnaps will not only tickle your recipients' tongues, but will fill their homes with the festive aroma of freshly baked cookies.

★ Christmas Gingersnaps

MAKES: 6 large jars, each with 12 cookies

⬜⬜⬜⬜⬜⬜

◔ **PREP TIME** 30 minutes, plus at least 4 hours to freeze
COOK TIME No cooking

INGREDIENTS:

4 cups all-purpose flour

2 teaspoons baking soda

1 teaspoon salt

2 tablepoons ground ginger

2 teaspoons ground cinnamon

1 teaspoon ground cloves

3 sticks unsalted butter, at room temperature

1 cup granulated sugar

1 cup packed dark brown sugar

2 large eggs

²/₃ cup molasses

2 cups raw brown sugar

1. Line two large baking cookie sheets with parchment paper.

2. Put the flour, baking soda, salt, ginger, cinnamon, and cloves into a medium bowl and mix to combine.

3. Put the butter, granulated sugar, and dark brown sugar into a large bowl and beat with an electric mixer until light and fluffy. Add the eggs and molasses and mix until incorporated. Add the flour mixture and beat until incorporated, scraping down the side of the bowl once or twice.

4. Put the raw brown sugar in a shallow bowl. Shape the dough into 1½-inch balls and roll in the sugar to coat completely. Place the balls on the prepared baking sheet spaced well apart. When the first sheet is full, use your fingertips to flatten the balls into circles about 3 inches in diameter (they should be about the same diameter as the canning jars) and ⅛ inch thick. If your fingers become too sticky, dip them in the sugar. Place the sheet in the freezer. Continue to shape the remaining dough until all the dough has been used and both sheets are full. Place the second sheet in the freezer and freeze for at least 4 hours or overnight, until the cookies are completely frozen.

5. Stack 12 frozen cookies in each of six 1-pint (16-fluid-ounce) widemouthed canning jars. Attach a gift tag to each jar with the following instructions:

How to bake Christmas Gingersnaps

Keep frozen. Preheat the oven to 350°F and place the cookies on an ungreased baking sheet. Bake in the preheated oven for 12–14 minutes, until the cookies are dry on the top and beginning to crisp. Remove from the oven and transfer to a cooling rack to cool. Serve at room temperature.

These decadent brownies beat a bought brownie mix any day.

Double Chocolate Brownie Mix

MAKES: 6 large jars, each with sufficient mix for 12 brownies

PREP TIME 10 minutes
COOK TIME No cooking

INGREDIENTS:

6 cups all-purpose flour

1½ teaspoons salt

3 cups packed light brown sugar

4 cups granulated sugar

4 cups unsweetened cocoa powder

3 cups chopped, toasted hazelnuts

3 cups mini semisweet chocolate chips

1. To prepare the gift jars, divide all of the ingredients evenly among six 1-pint (16-fluid-ounce) widemouthed canning jars. Add the ingredients in layers, starting with the flour. Place the lids on the jars and secure tightly.

2. Attach a gift tag to each jar with the following instructions:

How to prepare Double Chocolate Brownies

You will need:

2 large eggs

2 tablepoons milk

1 teaspoon vanilla extract

1 stick butter, melted, plus extra for greasing

Preheat the oven to 350°F and grease a 13 x 9-inch rectangular baking pan.

Transfer the brownie mix from the jar to a large mixing bowl. Put the eggs, milk, and vanilla extract into a separate bowl and mix to combine. Add the egg mixture to the dry ingredients and mix until well combined. Stir in the melted butter and mix to combine.

Transfer the batter to the prepared pan and bake in the preheated oven for about 20 minutes, or until the top is dry and a toothpick inserted into the center comes out almost clean. Place the pan on a cooling rack and let cool completely. Serve at room temperature.

1.   1.   1.

★ Cook's Tips ★

The brownie mix will keep for up to 6 months.
Cover tightly and store in a cool, dry place.

> **With just a few staples, this mix transforms into a delicious, nutritious breakfast treat.**

Cherry-Almond Muffin Mix

MAKES: 6 large jars, each with sufficient mix for 6 muffins

PREP TIME 10 minutes
COOK TIME No cooking

INGREDIENTS:

1½ cups packed light brown sugar

3 cups dried cherries

1½ cups granulated sugar

1½ cups ground almonds (almond meal)

4½ teaspoons baking powder

1½ teaspoons salt

4½ cups all-purpose flour

1. To prepare the gift jars, divide all of the ingredients evenly among six 1-pint (16-fluid-ounce) widemouthed canning jars. Add the ingredients in layers, starting with the sugar. Place the lids on the jars and secure tightly.

2. Attach a gift tag to each jar with the following instructions:

How to Bake Cherry-Almond Muffins

You will need:

2 large eggs, lightly beaten

½ cup milk

1 teaspoon vanilla extract or almond extract

1 stick unsalted butter, melted, plus extra for greasing (optional)

Preheat the oven to 350°F and lightly grease a 6-cup muffin pan or line with baking cups.

Transfer the muffin mix to a large bowl and stir to mix thoroughly. Put the eggs, milk, and vanilla extract into a small bowl and beat together. Add the egg mixture to the dry ingredients and mix with a wooden spoon until well combined. Add the butter and stir until combined.

Scoop the batter into the prepared pan. Bake in the preheated oven for 20–22 minutes, or until the tops are beginning to turn golden brown and a toothpick inserted into the center of a muffin comes out clean. Remove from the oven and transfer to a cooling rack to cool. Serve warm or at room temperature.

★ Cook's Tips ★

The muffin mix will keep for up to 6 months.
Seal tightly and store in a cool, dry place.

Blueberry Pancake Mix

There's no better way to wake up on a lazy Sunday than to homemade pancakes. Sweet yet tart dried blueberries and a hit of spicy cinnamon make these especially memorable.

MAKES: 6 large jars, each with sufficient mix for 2 servings

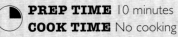 **PREP TIME** 10 minutes
COOK TIME No cooking

INGREDIENTS:

6 cups all-purpose flour

2 tablepoons baking powder

1 tablepoon baking soda

1 tablepoon salt

¾ cup granulated sugar

1 tablepoon ground cinnamon

¾ cup packed light brown sugar

1½ cups dried blueberries

¾ cup chopped pecans

1. To prepare the gift jars, divide all of the ingredients evenly among six 1-pint (16-fluid-ounce) widemouthed canning jars. Add the ingredients in layers, starting with the flour. Place the lids on the jars and secure tightly.

2. Attach a gift tag to each jar with the following instructions:

How to prepare Blueberry Pancakes

You will need:

½ cup buttermilk or milk

1 egg

1 tablepoon unsalted butter, melted, plus extra for cooking the pancakes

maple syrup, to serve

Put the buttermilk and the egg into a large bowl and whisk together. Add the mix from the jar and the butter and mix together well.

Melt a little butter in a skillet set over medium-high heat. Ladle the batter into the hot pan, about ¼ cup at a time. Cook for 2–3 minutes, until the bubbles that form on the top of the batter burst and aren't immediately filled by more batter. Flip the pancake and cook on the other side for an additional 2 minutes, or until golden brown. Continue until all of the batter has been used. Serve hot, drizzled with maple syrup.

★ Cook's Tips ★

This pancake mix will keep for up to 6 months.
Cover tightly and store in a cool, dry place.

★ Cook's Tips ★

The hot chocolate mix will keep for up to 6 months.
Cover tightly and store in a cool, dry place.

Crisp peppermint chocolate adds great flavor and a splash of color to a classic festive treat.

Indulgent Peppermint Hot Chocolate Mix

MAKES: 6 large jars, each with sufficient mix for 6 servings

PREP TIME 10 minutes
COOK TIME No cooking

INGREDIENTS:

6 cups instant dry milk

1½ cups unsweetened cocoa powder

1½ cups sugar

1½ cups mint chocolate chips

1. To prepare the gift jars, divide all of the ingredients evenly among six 1-pint (16-fluid-ounce) widemouthed canning jars. Add the ingredients in layers, starting with the dry milk. Place the lids on the jars and secure tightly.

2. Attach a tag to each jar with these instructions:

How to prepare Indulgent Peppermint Hot Chocolate

Pour the contents of the jar into a medium bowl and mix to combine. For each serving, put 3 tablespoons of the mix into a mug and add ¾ cup hot water or milk. Stir until the mix is completely dissolved. Serve immediately.

Herbed Beer Pretzel Mix

Attach a small, decorative bag filled with coarse salt or a small jar of mustard to complete this at-home snack-making kit.

MAKES: 6 large jars, each with sufficient mix for 8 pretzels

⬤ **PREP TIME** 10 minutes
⬤ **COOK TIME** No cooking

INGREDIENTS:

10½ cups all-purpose flour

3 tablepoons sugar

2 tablepoons plus ¾ teaspoon easy-blend active dry yeast

¼ cup dried thyme, rosemary, basil, or oregano

3 tablepoons salt

1. To prepare the gift jars, divide all of the ingredients evenly among six 1-pint (16-fluid-ounce) widemouthed canning jars. Add the ingredients in layers, starting with the flour. Place the lids on the jars and secure tightly.

2. Attach a gift label to each jar with these instructions:

How to Prepare Herbed Beer Pretzels

You will need:

¾ cup beer, at room temperature

1 tablepoon butter, melted

3–4 tablespoons all-purpose flour, plus extra for dusting

1 egg yolk, beaten with 1 tablepoon of water

coarse salt, for sprinkling

To prepare the pretzels, transfer the contents of the jar to a large mixing bowl. Add the beer and butter and mix until well combined. Add flour as needed, 1 tablespoon at a time, until the mixture is dry enough to knead with your hands (it should still be a bit sticky). Knead for several minutes until smooth. Place the dough in a large mixing bowl, cover with a clean dish towel, and let stand in a warm place for about 1 hour, until the dough has doubled in size.

Preheat the oven to 425°F and line a large baking sheet with parchment paper.

Turn out the dough onto a lightly floured board and divide into eight pieces. Roll each piece into a ball and then into a long sausage shape about 12 inches in length. Shape the lengths into pretzels and place on the prepared baking sheet.

Brush the tops of the pretzels with the egg-yolk mixture and sprinkle with the salt. Bake in the preheated oven for about 25 minutes, until the pretzels are golden brown. Remove from the oven and transfer to a cooling rack to cool. Serve warm or at room temperature.

★ Cook's Tips ★

The lentil soup mix will keep for up
to 6 months. Cover tightly and store
in a cool, dry place.

Give the gift of spicy, flavorful home-made soup that your recipients can enjoy any time they like.

Red Lentil Soup Mix

MAKES: 6 large jars, each with sufficient mix for 4 servings

PREP TIME 10 minutes
COOK TIME No cooking

INGREDIENTS:

4 cups dried red lentils

2 cups long-grain rice

¾ cup sun-dried tomatoes, finely chopped

¼ cup smoked paprika

2 tablepoons sweet paprika

2 tablepoons ground cumin

2 tablepoons salt

1 tablepoon garlic powder

1 tablepoon cayenne pepper

¾ cup instant chicken bouillon powder or instant vegetable bouillon powder

1. To prepare the gift jars, divide all of the ingredients evenly among six 1-pint (16-fluid-ounce) widemouthed canning jars. Add the ingredients in layers, starting with the lentils. Place the lids on the jars and secure tightly.

2. Attach a tag to each jar with the following instructions:

How to prepare Red Lentil Soup

You will need:

2 tablepoons olive oil

½ onion, diced

1 carrot, diced

1 celery stalk, diced

6 cups water

Heat the oil in a heavy saucepan over medium-high heat. Add the onion and cook, stirring, for about 5 minutes, until translucent. Add the carrot, celery, and the contents of the jar and cook, stirring, for an additional 1–2 minutes. Add the water, bring to a boil, reduce the heat to medium-low, and simmer for about 30–35 minutes, or until the rice and lentils are cooked through. Serve hot.

Index

This edition published by Parragon Books Ltd in 2013 and distributed by

Parragon Inc.
440 Park Avenue South, 13th Floor
New York, NY 10016
www.parragon.com/lovefood

LOVE FOOD is an imprint of Parragon Books Ltd

Copyright © Parragon Books Ltd 2013

LOVE FOOD and the accompanying heart device is a registered trademark of Parragon Books Ltd in the USA, the UK, Australia, India, and the EU.

ISBN 978-1-4723-2737-6

Printed in China

Project managed by Annabel King
Designed by Amy Child
Photography by Mike Cooper
Home economy by Lincoln Jefferson
New recipes by Robin Donovan
Edited by Fiona Biggs

Notes for the Reader
This book uses standard kitchen measuring spoons and cups. All spoon and cup measurements are level unless otherwise indicated. Unless otherwise stated, milk is assumed to be whole, eggs are large, individual vegetables are medium, and pepper is freshly ground black pepper. Unless otherwise stated, all root vegetables should be washed in plain water and peeled prior to using.

Garnishes, decorations, and serving suggestions are all optional and not necessarily included in the recipe ingredients or method. The times given are only an approximate guide. Preparation times differ according to the techniques used by different people and the cooking times may also vary from those given. Optional ingredients, variations, or serving suggestions have not been included in the time calculations.

Recipes using raw or very lightly cooked eggs should be avoided by infants, the elderly, pregnant women, convalescents, and anyone with a weakened immune system. Pregnant and breast-feeding women are advised to avoid eating peanuts and peanut products. People with nut allergies should be aware that some of the prepared ingredients used in the recipes in this book may contain nuts. Always check the packaging before use. Vegetarians should be aware that some of the prepared ingredients used in the recipes in this book may contain animal products. Always check the package before use.